Books by Willa Cather published by
the University of Nebraska Press

Alexander's Bridge

April Twilights, Revised Edition

The Autobiography of S. S. McClure

Death Comes for the Archbishop

The Kingdom of Art:
Willa Cather's First Principles and Critical Statements, 1893–1896

The Life of Mary Baker G. Eddy and the History of Christian Science
and Georgine Milmine

A Lost Lady

My Ántonia

Not Under Forty

O Pioneers!

Obscure Destinies

The Troll Garden: A Definitive Edition

Uncle Valentine and Other Stories:
Willa Cather's Uncollected Short Fiction, 1915–1929

Willa Cather in Europe:
Her Own Story of the First Journey

Willa Cather in Person:
Interviews, Speeches, and Letters

Willa Cather's Collected Short Fiction, 1892–1912

Willa Cather on Writing:
Critical Studies on Writing as an Art

WILLA CATHER

On Writing

Critical Studies on Writing as an Art

WITH A FOREWORD BY STEPHEN TENNANT

University of Nebraska Press
Lincoln and London

First Bison Book printing: 1988
Most recent printing indicated by the first digit below:

Library of Congress Cataloging-in-Publication Data

Cather, Willa, 1873–1947.
    On Writing: critical studies on writing as an art / Willa
Cather: with a foreword by Stephen Tennant.
        p.   cm.
Reprint. Originally published: New York: Knopf, c1920.
ISBN 0-8032-6332-5 (pbk.)
    1. Cather, Willa, 1873–1947—Aesthetics. 2. Literature—
History and criticism. I. Title. II. Title: Willa Cather on
writing.
PS3505.A87048   1988
813'.52—dc19   CIP 87-30078

Published by arrangement with Alfred A. Knopf, Inc.

THE ROOM BEYOND

A FOREWORD ON WILLA CATHER

In the glance that Willa Cather casts at her intention and achievement in the composition of *The Professor's House* she speaks of a Dutch interior, a drawing-room or kitchen, in which there is a window open, through which you see the masts of ships, or a strip of grey sea. There is for me a profound symbolism in this idea of seeing beyond the immediate room — either to sky or sea or mountains, or to the Room Beyond. Some of the Italian masters give vistas of colonnades or a balcony, a garden or a court. Willa Cather's art is essentially one of gazing beyond the immediate scene to a timeless sky or a timeless room, in which the future and the past, the unspoken and the unknown, forever beckon the happy reader.

That is why I have given to this Foreword the title of "The Room Beyond."

To write with the necessary detachment and circumspection of Willa Cather's critical essays (in this volume and in her *Not under Forty*) demands an approach at once laudatory and cautious. An artist of her vigour and individuality was bound to read the work of others with an exceptionally shrewd and discriminating eye.

It is important to stress the fact that her work as a critic sets her very much apart from other literary critics, on several counts.

She employed none of the usual jargon. Her mind was a stranger to the *déjà vue* and the *partis pris* attitudes so common in literary criticism. She possessed the ability to read the work of others with a child's crystalline vision, combined with a mature and seasoned wisdom quite her own, and extraordinarily beautiful in its quiet sureness.

Of course, in a sense she was incapable of divesting herself altogether of the creative writer's role. In many of these masterly essays one is

The Room Beyond

struck by the swift, benign way in which she devises and constructs a frame, a proscenium, in which her subjects shall function. She furnished and gave a window to the Room Beyond.

There we see that the great novelist was incapable of appraising starkly or bleakly any aspect of the subject she approached. Whether it be in "The Novel Démeublé," or "A Chance Meeting," or the Katherine Mansfield essay — the critical core of the work is always fledged round, circumscribed, and embellished by a rich romantic ambience — whose colour and music, veri-similitude and gay ardour, never threatened the drive and force of the writer's perspicacity.

It is Willa Cather's particular genius to reveal an even deeper awareness and significance in the finest work she criticizes. Her eye, her ear, were tuning-forks, burning-glasses, which caught the minutest refraction or echo of a thought or feeling. Often she delves deeper into a situation or predicament than the artist of whom she writes. She saw — into the Room Beyond.

A great critic is never limited by the ordinary

reader's more gullible eye. The tacit approach, the surface meaning — these were only obvious and often deceptive landmarks to Willa Cather. She heard a deeper vibration, a kind of composite echo, of all that the writer said, and did not say. Thus her critical essays are of inestimable value to the thoughtful reader, for they reveal new vistas of supposition and discovery in what appears a subject already totally appraised.

I should like to stress the particularly personal capacity for sympathy in this great writer and critic. One can say that the finest edge of her critical writing would have been powerless without the great range of her sympathies and ability to like, and divine, *Life* — even at its most grim and stark, — at its poorest and emptiest.

The wealth of her human warmth of feeling has been one of the great factors in the popularity of her books. It pervades everything — as fire pervades the center of the earth.

In the essay on Katherine Mansfield she adds an incomparable knowledge to our already strong appreciation of that delicate, searching talent —

The Room Beyond

which might so easily seem of too brittle a quality, or too ironic or whimsical or perverse in nature.

In "Prelude" and "To the Bay" we see, through Willa Cather's clear vision, the full power, beauty, and tragedy of the writer's life and work in all their most moving truth. I like to think that in the critic's profound analysis of Katherine Mansfield — in her total submersion in her subject — we see more clearly the great American novelist's most concentrated identity. The very absoluteness of her concentration in another artist's gifts liberates her own soul, her heart, with a most passionate clarity.

As a novelist, Willa Cather has a "naturalness" so great that one is tempted to think of her almost as not a writer at all. Her medium seems without category or label — and in saying this we pay her a very subtle compliment, for this rare and attaching naturalness has its birth in her deepest being — lies far below the surface of conscious endeavour.

It is the stamp of her unchallengeable integrity — and it animates her serene and often unstressed prose with a pure current of power.

As a critic she is more alert — never discursive — but more pungent in her approach. The detachment enjoyed by the critic evidently freed her pen from some tension, bordering on an onerous responsibility. Her critical essays are directed toward an ambiguous protagonist — a clever, vital, and interesting creature, who never gave her the burdensome sense of too placidly listening. It was like fencing, fine sword-work to her — and she adopts a glancing, resilient style in some of these essays which does suggest a master of acute and delicate swordsmanship. Writing a novel, although it schooled and tempered her artistry to a fine degree, gave a quietness, a subtone to her work, which is lacking in these crisp, vigorous, and sometimes great critical essays. One feels, reading "Escapism," her complete mastery of mood and diction. The equilibrium, equipoise, is a marvel of spontaneous wit and judicious, rallying bonhomie.

There is a kind of spiritual gaiety, of *joie de*

vivre and jubilation, in some of her essays which tempts one to think that there were more elements in Willa Cather's intellectual make-up than is usually suspected. She clearly possessed a talent for comedy — and much of the playwright's knowledge of the degree to which theatrical truth may be in advance of ordinary truth. The poet, the writer, knows that to produce an impression of veracity he must exaggerate. If the work is living stuff, with the passage of time this element of exaggeration — necessary to the work while in preparation — vanishes, and only the truth remains, the vital residuum.

Art is not life, and it is not a substitute for it, or an aggrandizement of a dubious reality. It is a necessary commodity — compacted of many realities and fantasies, unrealities and dreams, which the artist commands and respects. It is a method, the only one, of preserving the beauty of transient things, the wonder of youthful happiness, the pleasures of controversy, wit, and enterprise, and the finer aspects of intellectual discovery, in an enduring and pleasing form.

The Room Beyond

Willa Cather made of her art something very closely resembling life as we know it, but proof of her genius and artistry is the fact that she could transmute, with no apparent effort, the commonplaces of daily life — people — things — places — to an elixir that was, since it was art, essentially artificial. And I think elixir is the right word in this context, because the prevailing response, the emotion, she evoked in her readers was one of happiness.

We know she is a great writer, not because we feel that she deals with epic themes, passions at white heat, or noble dramas, but because of the curious fact that with a few mild sentences and rather uneventful narrative she convinces us that our own lives have given, and received, happiness. She reassures us of the importance of little things. The seemingly trivial events and emotions — these, by some oblique method never apparent on the surface, she makes momentous — vivid, more our own than our own often disguised and uncharacteristic lives. That is why her readers adore her; she restores to the ravaged ego its sense of unity — shall we say of *some* unity? — of a scheme, a final design in the rich, desolating chaos we call life.

The sympathy and eagerness underlying her work, her boundless zest for life, never blurred her awareness of the ugly, tawdry, cheap things. — Her greatness, for me, lies in the arrow-like flight of her faith in man ultimately — the eternal vision behind her work — juxtaposed to the homely, simple facts of life. She possessed, in addition to her artistry and craftsmanship, an extraordinary knowledge of what ordinary and extraordinary people feel and think in their daily lives. She understood the hearts of people — and wished always to understand them better. And her readers — with an unquestioning response — have given to her books the feeling she best loved to portray — a spontaneous warmth and generosity.

She is essentially a writer who is a eulogist of the simplest spirit in human kind. She portrayed many people, simple and complex, with a generous amplitude of understanding. Yet she was not deluded or duped by human nature. Perhaps her greatness is partly the power to comprehend fully and yet *love* people, and value them.

She could portray young hearts, *young longing,* as very few artists have ever done. Perhaps Tolstoi has done this sometimes; but she did not use his elaboration or irony. She was curiously independent in all her approaches. Her vision was a poet's vision, simplified by an extraordinary natural honesty and warmth.

When one thinks of the deep, indelible impression made by some of her books — *A Lost Lady, My Mortal Enemy, My Ántonia* — I think it is the burden of unspent feeling one remembers; something gathered up, inviolably, delicately, almost denied one.

She loved faithfulness. It was her preferred climate. It was a climate in which she could breathe. She understood it as perhaps only a rare poet, a pioneer, can. She gives the impression of one who has gazed deep and long into the crystal of human fidelity.

Even when she is not dealing directly with loyalty or fine character, solidarity or honesty, she

The Room Beyond

has a way of reminding us that these form the cornerstones of her spiritual edifice. Her reader is never in doubt as to the nobleness of his ultimate choice. And Willa Cather's nobility is of a very curious kind. There is no compulsion, no dogma or creed behind this unwavering vision — a vision as level and wide as the landscapes and skyscapes of the West. She never inveigles or compromises her listener. If power can be abstract, hers is. Yet he swears allegiance, her hold is the stronger for being purely a magnetic "pull." No reader was ever more free, more utterly at liberty — to roam, escape, explore, sleep or wake — than this one.

One might say that a fine novel is like a life you lead. Readers felt that they could lead this wonderful, vicarious life with absolute trust, enjoyment, and exhilaration, because the unseen and even forgotten writer bore the stamp of an implicit integrity. A great writer should always have an anonymous quality, something remote like a pregnant silence — which is silent, and yet contains all sound, all time, all things. Her readers took her hand in loving trust, then forgot that they were holding anyone's hand. It was simply life. Virginia Woolf wrote in an essay: "With certain writers we feel, 'Yes, life is like that.' " — We are assuaged, appeased, by a sense of security and belief.

All human beings are egoists, and I believe that what attaches us to a writer we admire is a profound sense of affinity, of resemblance to ourselves — also a sharing of our dilemmas and predicaments. The great writer assuages and palliates some unanalysable loneliness that lies deep within each human soul. After childhood and adolescence all human creatures suffer from a certain unsureness, born of what is commonly called an adult understanding of life, but which is in reality an amorphous indefinite hinterland of self-distrust and ignorance. The great writers give us direction, motive, the power to assimilate wisdom and knowledge. They hearten us and reinforce our belief that life is rich, curious, and inexhaustible.

The concept of the Room Beyond applies inversely to her destructive criticism at its finest.

The Room Beyond

In her preface to Daniel Defoe's *Roxana* we see her scalpel finely cutting beyond the preconceived notion of Defoe's celebrated story of a courtesan. With no effort or ingenuity she lays bare the fundamental aridity, the paucity of feeling in this work. She grants him verisimilitude and a certain kind of drab and mercenary truthfulness; but how stark is the picture she leaves of Defoe and his creatures! How unassailable her verdict is! In sure and eviscerating sentences she picks to the bare bones of the book, and leaves finally only its basic structure — to whimper in the wind of ignoring time. One never has the sense of a mischievous pleasure in destruction in this essay. Willa Cather's greatness is never more in evidence than when she damns! It interests her only for the sake of truth. And her warm and compelling accents almost belie the censure of her words. She flashes such a warm and benignant glance over the gold-veined rocks of this sere mining country — where only gold is mined, at the price of all else — that it is difficult to realize fully how destructive her words are. And yet we know by the unerring light of her critical beam that this is a soulless book — a vigorous circumstantial record of utterly worthless people, who have lived in vain.

Few critical essays ever had a finer "curtain" (to take an expression from the theatre) than the last sentence of this essay. Speaking of *Robinson Crusoe* and *Roxana*, the writer says:

"The one book has what Stevenson called charm of circumstance, the other emphatically has not; but in both the same nature is effectually asserting itself; mean enough and vital enough — invulnerable because it never affects qualities which it neither comprehends nor admires."

Reading these essays we feel that poetic warmth and generosity of the writer's vision, her gaze, as she turns it upon man and art. Critical values are controversial — they must remain, up to a point, open to question; but these essays have an imponderable gravity and radiance, excelling and surpassing the immediate pleasure they give. Opinions will always vary and fluctuate on the absorbing subject of art — literary genius and composition; but I think Willa Cather's contribution is immortal in its aura and substance. Very few writers have ever so satisfactorily fused the factual and the visionary in one critical approach.

Her judgment is never subordinated to her sympathies. Much of her strength lies in the ability to canalize, in perfect language, a complexity of emotions — to weigh delicately and shrewdly the essential virtues in a writer or critic or a work. There was no indecision, no hesitancy in Willa Cather's stringent viewpoint. Her critical gaze was never coloured or deflected by irrelevant circumstance. The interest is always centralized.

The essay on Miss Jewett is one of the finest in this collection. It can be read simply for the delight it gives, — the pure enjoyment that eschews analysis. Or it can be read for the directness of its approach to a certain aspect of American life, New England sixty years ago, surely and serenely appraised, viewed in connection with Miss Jewett's delicate, unique books. Or again it can be read for the penetrating wisdom of its unconscious philosophy, its enduring values. Willa Cather's moral judgment is always a stimulant — never a depleting force.

One hesitates to speak, in this context, of anything so trite as a philosophy of life; it seems stereotyped, but in this case it is peculiarly pertinent. Miss Jewett's stories evoked in Willa Cather a complexity of rich responses — one of the predominating ones being a moral response, closely related to her philosophy of life. In this essay she defines her critical preferences, her moral preferences — shall we call it her fastidious response to the finest art in writing? — with a memorable finality.

The values by which she lived and wrote are particularly needed by the world today, to remind people that there are values and standards which time does not weaken. Work like hers, reflecting so truly human character and predicament, has a perennial bearing on existence — a vital bearing that strengthens with the passage of time. Her magnanimity and tolerance are born from her art and from her life. They are more valuable be-

The Room Beyond

cause they are so instinctive and spontaneous. Willa Cather taught the best of all philosophies, that of love and enterprise and courage.

I always find it difficult to reconcile the sternness of her æsthetic preferences, the exclusiveness of her taste, with the unhampered zest for enjoyment, the warmth of her pleasure in writing that pleased her. She is implacable in her judgments, yet she is never narrow, never chilled by what is unimportant — or, indeed, at all concerned with trivial work. Much of her greatness as a writer lies in this dual capacity: the ability to reject, unreservedly, anything mediocre or shoddy — and a pure unalloyed delight in the fine and sincere. Her guiding voice as a critic gives to this book a triumphant dignity, a beauty unique in our time.

There can be few great short stories as engrossing as "A Chance Meeting" (in the volume *Not under Forty*). It possesses the qualities of the rarest fiction, allied to the compelling interest of a factual incident. One can never exhaust the subtle joys of this exquisite essay. Like all great work, it holds something in the future, unspent.

The Room Beyond

It is as diverting as a good play, as haunting as great music — and for each reader it has a unique contribution, the responsiveness of a living thing.

Alexander's Bridge, Willa Cather's first novel, to which she refers in one of these studies, is particularly interesting for the sense of potential power that it holds. All the books that were yet unwritten are implicit in the narrative of this intensely felt short novel. It is explosive with the riches to come. And it is very finely constructed and admirably written; a serene vitality pervades its pages. You have the impression of a writer at peace with his theme and his treatment. The sadness of this book is the sadness of real life. A love story, told with great power and restraint, and tragic with the tragedy that is unalterable.

Willa Cather speaks of *Alexander's Bridge* with only toleration, — but I like to see it as an interesting link in the chain of her books.

The *Novel Démeublé* is the most cogent and salient essay in this volume. It is a concentrated exposition of the novelist's art — provocative,

The Room Beyond

richly dynamic, — an essential note to be kept on the young writer's work-table, to remind him of the ever present dangers and delights of literary composition.

Readers who have loved her novels will feel, reading these critical essays, a renewed joy in her serene, pellucid prose style, her noble and original mind.

Willa Cather is particularly cogent and entertaining in the letters and notes concerning her own books. Her comments, her analyses, are those of the poet. They are never fluent or highly coloured. Yet she delights the reader with the deepest kind of quiet joy — almost like self-realization, an intensification of some sure self-knowledge, which, in its turn, illumines life, and the august, ravaged, and exalted past, in a clear light.

One is again reminded of the breadth of her critical vision, its lambent warmth and tireless curiosity about human behaviour and circumstance.

It is her particular gift to reveal the reader's

finest being to his own cognizance and to bring the outer world, daily life, casual experience, into a curiously close relation to this self-knowledge.

A great writer is always an influence of expansion. He gives direction to the reader's thoughts. The world is more interesting when it is viewed by a subtle and invigorating mind that deals summarily with the inessentials, and lays bare in all their fascination and glory the great truths, the deathless power that is in man, and in his irreducible and ever changing eternity.

STEPHEN TENNANT

New York . . . Sarasota
March 1949

CONTENTS

FOUR LETTERS

ON

DEATH COMES FOR THE ARCHBISHOP

Unable to reply personally to the hundreds of letters Miss Cather received asking her in how far Death Comes for the Archbishop *was historical, and what were her sources of information, she wrote the following letter to* The Commonweal:

To THE EDITOR OF *The Commonweal:* — You have asked me to give you a short account of how I happened to write *Death Comes for the Archbishop.*

When I first went into the Southwest some

fifteen years ago, I stayed there for a considerable period of time. It was then much harder to get about than it is today. There were no automobile roads and no hotels off the main lines of railroad. One had to travel by wagon and carry a camp outfit. One travelled slowly, and had plenty of time for reflection. It was then very difficult to find anyone who would tell me anything about the country, or even about the roads. One of the most intelligent and inspiriting persons I found in my travels was a Belgian priest, Father Halter-mann, who lived with his sister in the parsonage behind the beautiful old church at Santa Cruz, New Mexico, where he raised fancy poultry and sheep and had a wonderful vegetable and flower garden. He was a florid, full-bearded farmer priest, who drove about among his eighteen Indian missions with a spring wagon and a pair of mules. He knew a great deal about the country and the Indians and their traditions. He went home during the war to serve as a chaplain in the French Army, and when I last heard of him he was an invalid.

On Death Comes for the Archbishop

The longer I stayed in the Southwest, the more I felt that the story of the Catholic Church in that country was the most interesting of all its stories. The old mission churches, even those which were abandoned and in ruins, had a moving reality about them; the hand-carved beams and joists, the utterly unconventional frescoes, the countless fanciful figures of the saints, no two of them alike, seemed a direct expression of some very real and lively human feeling. They were all fresh, individual, first-hand. Almost every one of those many remote little adobe churches in the mountains or in the desert had something lovely that was its own. In lonely, sombre villages in the mountains the church decorations were sombre, the martyrdoms bloodier, the grief of the Virgin more agonized, the figure of Death more terrifying. In warm, gentle valleys everything about the churches was milder. I used to wish there were some written account of the old times when those churches were built; but I soon felt that no record of them could be as real as they are themselves. They are their own story, and it is foolish convention that we must have everything interpreted for us in written language. There are other ways of telling what one feels, and the people who built and decorated those many, many little churches found their way and left their message.

May I say here that within the last few years some of the newer priests down in that country have been taking away from those old churches their old homely images and decorations, which have a definite artistic and historic value, and replacing them by conventional, factory-made church furnishings from New York? It is a great pity. All Catholics will be sorry about it, I think, when it is too late, when all those old paintings and images and carved doors that have so much feeling and individuality are gone — sold to some collector in New York or Chicago, where they mean nothing.

During the twelve years that followed my first year in New Mexico and Arizona I went back as often as I could, and the story of the Church and the Spanish missionaries was always what most interested me; but I hadn't the most remote idea of trying to write about it. I was working on things of a very different nature, and any story of the Church in the Southwest was certainly the business of some Catholic writer, and not mine at all.

Meanwhile Archbishop Lamy, the first Bishop of New Mexico, had become a sort of invisible personal friend. I had heard a great many interesting stories about him from very old Mexicans and traders who still remembered him, and I never passed the life-size bronze of him which stands under a locust tree before the Cathedral in Santa Fé without wishing that I could learn more about a pioneer churchman who looked so well-bred and distinguished. In his pictures one felt the same thing, something fearless and fine and very, very well-bred — something that spoke of race. What I felt curious about was the daily life of such a man in a crude frontier society.

Two years ago, in Santa Fé, that curiosity was gratified. I came upon a book printed years ago on a country press at Pueblo, Colorado: *The Life of the Right Reverend Joseph P. Machebeuf,* by William Joseph Howlett, a priest who had worked with Father Machebeuf in Denver. The book is an admirable piece of work, revealing as much about Father Lamy as about Father Machebeuf, since the two men were so closely associated from early youth. Father Howlett had gone to France and got his information about Father Machebeuf's youth direct from his sister, Philomene. She gave him her letters from Father Machebeuf, telling all the little details of his life in New Mexico, and Father Howlett inserted dozens of them, splendidly translated, into his biography. At last I found out what I wanted to know about how the country and the people of New Mexico seemed to those first missionary priests from France. Without these letters in Father Howlett's book to guide me, I would certainly never have dared to write my book. Of course, many of the incidents I used were experiences of my own, but in these letters I learned how experiences very similar to them affected Father Machebeuf and Father Lamy.

My book was a conjunction of the general and the particular, like most works of the imagination. I had all my life wanted to do something in the style of legend, which is absolutely the reverse of dramatic treatment. Since I first saw the Puvis de Chavannes frescoes of the life of Saint Geneviève in my student days, I have wished that I could try something a little like that in prose; something without accent, with none of the artificial elements of composition. In the Golden Legend the martyrdoms of the saints are no more dwelt upon than are the trivial incidents of their lives; it is as though all human experiences, measured against one supreme spiritual experience, were of about the same importance. The essence of such writing is not to hold the note, not to use an incident for all there is in it — but to touch and pass on. I felt that such writing would be a kind of discipline in these days when the "situation" is made to count for so much in writing,

Four Letters

when the general tendency is to force things up. In this kind of writing the mood is the thing — all the little figures and stories are mere improvisations that come out of it. What I got from Father Machebeuf's letters was the mood, the spirit in which they accepted the accidents and hardships of a desert country, the joyful energy that kept them going. To attempt to convey this hardihood of spirit one must use language a little stiff, a little formal, one must not be afraid of the old trite phraseology of the frontier. Some of those time-worn phrases I used as the note from the piano by which the violinist tunes his instrument. Not that there was much difficulty in keeping the pitch. I did not sit down to write the book until the feeling of it had so teased me that I could not get on with other things. The writing of it took only a few months, because the book had all been lived many times before it was written, and the happy mood in which I began it never paled. It was like going back and playing the early composers after a surfeit of modern music.

One friendly reviewer says that to write the

book I soaked myself in Catholic lore; perhaps it would have been better if I had. But too much information often makes one pompous, and it's rather deadening. Some things I had to ask about. I had no notion of the manner in which a missionary from the new world would be received by the Pope, so I simply asked an old friend, Father Dennis Fitzgerald, the resident priest in Red Cloud, Nebraska, where my parents live. He was a student in Rome in his youth, so I asked him to tell me something about the procedure of a formal audience with the Pope. There again I had to exercise self-restraint, for he told me such interesting things that I was strongly tempted to make Father Vaillant's audience stand out too much, to particularize it. Knowledge that one hasn't got first-hand is a dangerous thing for a writer, it comes too easily!

Writing this book (the title, by the way, which has caused a good deal of comment, was simply taken from Holbein's *Dance of Death*) was like a happy vacation from life, a return to childhood, to early memories. As a writer I had the satisfaction of working in a special genre which I had long wished to try. As a human being, I had the pleasure of paying an old debt of gratitude to the valiant men whose life and work had given me so many hours of pleasant reflection in far-away places where certain unavoidable accidents and physical discomforts gave me a feeling of close kinship with them. In the main, I followed the life story of the two Bishops very much as it was, though I used many of my own experiences, and some of my father's. In actual fact, of course, Bishop Lamy died first of the two friends, and it was Bishop Machebeuf who went to his funeral. Often have I heard from the old people how he broke down when he rose to speak and was unable to go on.

I am amused that so many of the reviews of this book begin with the statement: "This book is hard to classify." Then why bother? Many more assert vehemently that it is not a novel. Myself, I prefer to call it a narrative. In this case I think that term more appropriate. But a novel, it seems to me, is merely a work of imagination in

On Death Comes for the Archbishop

which a writer tries to present the experiences and emotions of a group of people by the light of his own. That is what he really does, whether his method is "objective" or "subjective."

I hope that I have told you what you wished to know about my book, and I remain,

Very sincerely yours,

Willa Cather

November 23, 1927

In his review of *Death Comes for the Archbishop*, Michael Williams wrote in *The Commonweal*:

"Her [Willa Cather's] book is a wonderful proof of the power of the true artist to penetrate and understand and to express things not part of the equipment of the artist as a person. Miss Cather is not a Catholic, yet certainly no Catholic American writer that I know of has ever written so many pages so steeped in spiritual knowledge and understanding of Catholic motives and so sympathetically illustrative of the wonder and beauty of Catholic mysteries, as she has done in this book."

ON

SHADOWS ON THE ROCK

Shortly after Shadows on the Rock *was published, Miss Cather wrote to Governor Wilbur
Cross of Connecticut in acknowledgment of his
appreciative review of the book, which appeared
in* The Saturday Review of Literature. *Later the
editor of the* Saturday Review *obtained permission from Governor Cross and Miss Cather to
publish this letter in the* Review.

DEAR GOVERNOR CROSS: —

I want to thank you most heartily for the most
understanding review I have seen of my new
book. You seem to have seen what a different
kind of method I tried to use from that which

On Shadows on the Rock

I used in the *Archbishop*. I tried, as you say, to
state the mood and the viewpoint in the title. To
me the rock of Quebec is not only a stronghold
on which many strange figures have for a little
time cast a shadow in the sun; it is the curious
endurance of a kind of culture, narrow but definite. There another age persists. There, among
the country people and the nuns, I caught something new to me; a kind of feeling about life and
human fate that I could not accept, wholly, but
which I could not but admire. It is hard to state
that feeling in language; it was more like an old
song, incomplete but uncorrupted, than like a
legend. The text was mainly anacoluthon, so to
speak, but the meaning was clear. I took the incomplete air and tried to give it what would cor-
respond to a sympathetic musical setting; tried to
develop it into a prose composition not too con-
clusive, not too definite: a series of pictures remembered rather than experienced; a kind of
thinking, a mental complexion inherited, left
over from the past, lacking in robustness and full
of pious resignation.

Four Letters

Now, it seemed to me that the mood of the misfits among the early settlers (and there were a good many) must have been just that. An orderly little French household that went on trying to live decently, just as ants begin to rebuild when you kick their house down, interests me more than Indian raids or the wild life in the forests. And, as you seem to recognize, once having adopted a tone so definite, once having taken your seat in the close air by the apothecary's fire, you can't explode into military glory, any more than you can pour champagne into a salad dressing. (I don't believe much in rules, but Stevenson laid down a good one when he said: *You can't mix kinds.*) And really, a new society begins with the salad dressing more than with the destruction of Indian villages. Those people brought a kind of French culture there and somehow kept it alive on that rock, sheltered it and tended it and on occasion died for it, as if it really were a sacred fire — and all this temperately and shrewdly, with emotion always tempered by good sense.

On Shadows on the Rock

It's very hard for an American to catch that rhythm — it's so unlike us. But I made an honest try, and I got a great deal of pleasure out of it, if nobody else does! And surely you'll agree with me that our writers experiment too little, and produce their own special brand too readily.

With deep appreciation of the compliment you pay me in taking the time to review the book, and my friendliest regards always,

Faithfully,

Willa Cather

Published in The Saturday Review of Literature, October 17, 1931.

ESCAPISM

A *Letter to* The Commonweal

My Dear Mr. Williams:

You were asking me what I thought about a new term in criticism: the Art of "Escape." Isn't the phrase tautological? What has art ever been but escape? To be sure, this definition is for the moment used in a derogatory sense, implying an evasion of duty, something like the behaviour of a poltroon. When the world is in a bad way, we are told, it is the business of the composer and the poet to devote himself to propaganda and fan the flames of indignation.

Escapism

But the world has a habit of being in a bad way from time to time, and art has never contributed anything to help matters — except escape. Hundreds of years ago, before European civilization had touched this continent, the Indian women in the old rock-perched pueblos of the Southwest were painting geometrical patterns on the jars in which they carried water up from the streams. Why did they take the trouble? These people lived under the perpetual threat of drought and famine; they often shaped their graceful cooking pots when they had nothing to cook in them. Anyone who looks over a collection of prehistoric Indian pottery dug up from old burial-mounds knows at once that the potters experimented with form and colour to gratify something that had no concern with food and shelter. The major arts (poetry, painting, architecture, sculpture, music) have a pedigree all their own. They did not come into being as a means of increasing the game supply or promoting tribal security. They sprang from an unaccountable predilection of the one unaccountable thing in man.

Four Letters

At the moment, we hear the same cry which went up during the French Revolution: the one really important thing for every individual is his citizenship, his loyalty to a cause — which, of course, always means his loyalty to a party. The composer should be Citizen Beethoven, the painter Citizen Rembrandt, the poet Citizen Shelley, and they should step into line and speed their pen or brush in helping to solve the economic problems which confront society. There have been generous and bold spirits among the artists: Courbet tried to kick down the Vendôme Column and got himself exiled, Citizen Shelley stepped into line and drove his pen — but he was not very useful to the reforms which fired his imagination. He was "useful," if you like that word, only as all true poets are, because they refresh and recharge the spirit of those who can read their language.

"Face the stern realities, you skulking Escapist!" the Radical editor cries. Yes, but usually the poor Escapist has so little cleverness when he struggles with stern realities. Schubert could easily write a dozen songs a day, but he couldn't keep himself in shirts. Suppose the Radical editor, or the head of the Works Project, had to write a dozen songs a day? I can't believe that if Tolstoi and Goethe and Viollet-le-Duc and Descartes and Sir Isaac Newton were brought together and induced to work with a will, their opinions, voiced in their various special languages and formulæ, would materially help Mayor La Guardia to better living conditions in New York City. Nearly all the Escapists in the long past have managed their own budget and their social relations so unsuccessfully that I wouldn't want them for my landlords, or my bankers, or my neighbours. They were valuable, like powerful stimulants, only when they were left out of the social and industrial routine which goes on every day all over the world. Industrial life has to work out its own problems.

Give the people a new word, and they think they have a new fact. The pretentious-sounding noun Escapist isn't even new. Just now, it is applied to writers with more acrimony than to composers or sculptors. Since poets and novelists do not speak in symbols or a special language, but in the plain speech which all men use and all men may, after some fashion, read, they are told that their first concern should be to cry out against social injustice. This, of course, writers have always done. The Hebrew prophets and the Greek dramatists went deeper; they considered the greed and selfishness innate in every individual; the valour which leads to power, and the tyranny which power begets. They even cried out against the seeming original injustice that creatures so splendidly aspiring should be inexorably doomed to fail; the unfairness of the contest in which beings whose realest life is in thought or endeavour are kept always under the shackles of their physical body, and are, as Ulysses said, "the slaves of the belly." Since no patriarchal family was without its hatreds and jealousies and treacheries, the old poets could not see how a great number of families brought together into a State could be much better. This seems to be the writer's natural way of looking at the suffering of the world.

Escapism

Seventy-five years ago Dostoievsky was the idol of the Revolutionary party; but who could now consider his novels propaganda? Certainly they are very unlike the product of the young man who goes to spend a year in a factory town and writes a novel on the abuses of factory labour.

Why does the man who wants to reform industrial conditions so seldom follow the method of the pamphleteers? Only by that method can these subjects be seriously and fairly discussed. And the people who are able to do anything toward improving such conditions will read only such a discussion: they will take little account of facts presented in a coating of stock cinema situations.

Why do the propagandists use a vehicle which they consider rickety and obsolete, to convey a message which they believe all-important? When I first lived in New York and was working on the editorial staff of a magazine, I became disillusioned about social workers and reformers. So many of them, when they brought in an article on fire-trap tenements or sweat-shop labour, apologetically explained that they were making these investigations "to collect material for fiction." I couldn't believe that any honest welfare worker, or any honest novelist, went to work in this way. The man who wants to get reforms put through does his investigating in a very different spirit, and the man who has a true vocation for imaginative writing doesn't have to go hunting among the ash cans on Sullivan Street for his material. There were exceptions to these double-purposed, faltering soldiers of good causes — and the exceptions were splendid. The exceptions nearly always are. And their exceptionalness, oftener than not, comes not only from a superior endowment, but from a deeper purpose, and a willingness to pay the cost instead of being paid for it.

But doesn't the new social restlessness spring from a desire to do away with the exceptional? And isn't this desire partly the result of thwarted ambitions? Eighteen or twenty years ago there were graduated from our universities a company of unusually promising men, who were also extravagantly ambitious. The world was changing, and they meant to play a conspicuous part in this change: to make a new kind of thought and a new kind of expression; in language, color, form, sound. They were to bring about a renaissance within a decade or so. Failing in this, they made a career of destroying the past. The only new thing they offered us was contempt for the old. Then began the flood of belittling biography which has poured over us ever since. We were told how shallow had been all the great philosophers, what educated dullards were Goethe, Rousseau, Spinoza, Pascal. Shakespeare and Dante were easily disposed of; the one because he was somebody else, the other because he was a cryptogram and did not at all mean to say what the greatest lines in the Italian language make him say. Able research work was done on the bodily diseases and physical imperfections of Beethoven, Schubert, Hugo Wolf, and all the German composers. Not even their teeth were overlooked.

Is this a natural, unprejudiced way to study history? What does it lead to? Nothing very worthy. And what it comes from is less worthy still.

Some of these iconoclasts and tomb-breakers were undoubtedly sincere. They attacked the old popular heroes in a spirit of dreary hopelessness rather than with a disgust bred of the chagrin from disappointed ambitions. The false past must be destroyed, they said, before the new and the true can be born.

Not at all: spare yourselves that disagreeable duty. Give us a new work of genius of any kind, and if it is alive, and fired with some more vital feeling than contempt, you will see how automatically the old and false makes itself air before the new and true.

The revolt against individualism naturally calls artists severely to account, because the artist is of all men the most individual: those who were not have been long forgotten. The condition every art requires is, not so much freedom from restriction, as freedom from adulteration and from the intrusion of foreign matter; considerations and purposes which have nothing to do with spontaneous invention. The great body of Russian literature was produced when the censorship was at its strictest. The art of Italy flowered when the painters were confined almost entirely to religious subjects. In the great age of Gothic architecture sculptors and stone-cutters told the same stories (with infinite variety and fresh invention) over and over, on the faces of all the cathedrals and churches of Europe. How many clumsy experiments in government, futile revolutions and reforms, those buildings have looked down upon without losing a shadow of their dignity and power — of their importance! Religion and art spring from the same root and are close kin. Economics and art are strangers.

The literary radicals tell us there must be a new kind of poetry. There will be, whenever there is a new poet — a genuine one. The thesis that no one can ever write a noble sonnet on a noble theme without repeating Wordsworth, or a mysteriously lovely lyric without repeating Shelley, is an evasion. As well argue that because so many thumb-prints have already been taken, there must be a new method of identification. No fine poet can ever write like another. His poetry is simply his individuality. And the themes of true poetry, of great poetry, will be the same until all the values of human life have changed and all the strongest emotional responses have become different — which can hardly occur until the physical body itself has fundamentally changed.

So far, the effort to make a new kind of poetry, "pure poetry," which eschews (or renounces) the old themes as shop-worn, and confines itself to regarding the grey of a wet oyster shell against the sand of a wet beach through a drizzle of rain, has not produced anything very memorable: not even when the workmanship was good and when a beat in the measure was unexpectedly dropped here and there with what one of the poet's admirers calls a "heart-breaking effect." Certainly the last thing such poetry should attempt is to do any heart-breaking.

Now, my dear Mr. Williams, I have already said much too much about a fleeting fashion which perhaps is not to be taken seriously at all.

Escapism

As Mary Colum remarked in the *Yale Review*: "The people who talk about the art of escape simply know nothing about art at all." At *all*, I echo!

Sincerely yours,

Willa Cather

April 17, 1936

ON

THE PROFESSOR'S HOUSE

*These paragraphs from a letter to a friend were
printed, with Miss Cather's permission, in the
News Letter.*

. . . Let me try to answer your question. When
I wrote *The Professor's House*, I wished to try
two experiments in form. The first is the device
often used by the early French and Spanish novelists; that of inserting the *Nouvelle* into the *Ro-
man.* "Tom Outland's Story" has been published
in French and Polish and Dutch, as a short narrative for school children studying English.

On The Professor's House

But the experiment which interested me was something a little more vague, and was very much akin to the arrangement followed in sonatas in which the academic sonata form was handled somewhat freely. Just before I began the book I had seen, in Paris, an exhibition of old and modern Dutch paintings. In many of them the scene presented was a living-room warmly furnished, or a kitchen full of food and coppers. But in most of the interiors, whether drawing-room or kitchen, there was a square window, open, through which one saw the masts of ships, or a stretch of grey sea. The feeling of the sea that one got through those square windows was remarkable, and gave me a sense of the fleets of Dutch ships that ply quietly on all the waters of the globe — to Java, etc.

In my book I tried to make Professor St. Peter's house rather overcrowded and stuffy with new things; American proprieties, clothes, furs, petty ambitions, quivering jealousies — until one got rather stifled. Then I wanted to open the square window and let in the fresh air that blew off the

Four Letters

Blue Mesa, and the fine disregard of trivialities which was in Tom Outland's face and in his behaviour.

The above concerned me as a writer only, but the Blue Mesa (the Mesa Verde) actually was discovered by a young cowpuncher in just this way. The great explorer Nordenskjöld wrote a scientific book about this discovery, and I myself had the good fortune to hear the story of it from a very old man, brother of Dick Wetherell. Dick Wetherell as a young boy forded Mancos River and rode into the Mesa after lost cattle. I followed the real story very closely in Tom Outland's narrative.

Willa Cather

December 12, 1938

THE NOVEL DÉMEUBLÉ

THE NOVEL DÉMEUBLÉ

The novel, for a long while, has been over-furnished. The property-man has been so busy on its pages, the importance of material objects and their vivid presentation have been so stressed, that we take it for granted whoever can observe, and can write the English language, can write a novel. Often the latter qualification is considered unnecessary.

In any discussion of the novel, one must make it clear whether one is talking about the novel as a form of amusement, or as a form of art; since they serve very different purposes and in very different ways. One does not wish the egg one eats for breakfast, or the morning paper, to be made of the stuff of immortality. The novel manufactured to entertain great multitudes of people must be considered exactly like a cheap soap or a cheap perfume, or cheap furniture. Fine quality is a distinct disadvantage in articles made for great numbers of people who do not want quality but quantity, who do not want a thing that "wears," but who want change, — a succession of new things that are quickly threadbare and can be lightly thrown away. Does anyone pretend that if the Woolworth store windows were piled high with Tanagra figurines at ten cents, they could for a moment compete with Kewpie brides in the popular esteem? Amusement is one thing; enjoyment of art is another.

Every writer who is an artist knows that his "power of observation," and his "power of description," form but a low part of his equipment. He must have both, to be sure; but he knows that the most trivial of writers often have a very good observation. Mérimée said in his remarkable essay on Gogol: "L'art de choisir parmi les innombrables traits que nous offre la nature est, après tout, bien plus difficile que celui de les observer avec attention et de les rendre avec exactitude."

There is a popular superstition that "realism" asserts itself in the cataloguing of a great number of material objects, in explaining mechanical processes, the methods of operating manufactories and trades, and in minutely and unsparingly describing physical sensations. But is not realism, more than it is anything else, an attitude of mind on the part of the writer toward his material, a vague indication of the sympathy and candour with which he accepts, rather than chooses, his theme? Is the story of a banker who is unfaithful to his wife and who ruins himself by speculation in trying to gratify the caprices of his mistresses, at all reinforced by a masterly exposition of banking, our whole system of credits, the methods of the Stock Exchange? Of course, if the story is thin, these things do reinforce it in a sense, — any amount of red meat thrown into the scale to make the beam dip. But are the banking

The Novel Démeublé

system and the Stock Exchange worth being written about at all? Have such things any proper place in imaginative art?

The automatic reply to this question is the name of Balzac. Yes, certainly, Balzac tried out the value of literalness in the novel, tried it out to the uttermost, as Wagner did the value of scenic literalness in the music drama. He tried it, too, with the passion of discovery, with the inflamed zest of an unexampled curiosity. If the heat of that furnace could not give hardness and sharpness to material accessories, no other brain will ever do it. To reproduce on paper the actual city of Paris; the houses, the upholstery, the food, the wines, the game of pleasure, the game of business, the game of finance: a stupendous ambition — but, after all, unworthy of an artist. In exactly so far as he succeeded in pouring out on his pages that mass of brick and mortar and furniture and proceedings in bankruptcy, in exactly so far he defeated his end. The things by which he still lives, the types of greed and avarice and ambition and vanity and lost innocence of heart which he

The Novel Démeublé

created — are as vital today as they were then. But their material surroundings, upon which he expended such labour and pains . . . the eye glides over them. We have had too much of the interior decorator and the "romance of business" since his day. The city he built on paper is already crumbling. Stevenson said he wanted to blue-pencil a great deal of Balzac's "presentation" — and he loved him beyond all modern novelists. But where is the man who could cut one sentence from the stories of Mérimée? And who wants any more detail as to how Carmencita and her fellow factory-girls made cigars? Another sort of novel? Truly. Isn't it a better sort?

In this discussion another great name naturally occurs. Tolstoi was almost as great a lover of material things as Balzac, almost as much interested in the way dishes were cooked, and people were dressed, and houses were furnished. But there is this determining difference: the clothes, the dishes, the haunting interiors of those old Moscow houses, are always so much a part of the emotions of the people that they are perfectly synthesized; they seem to exist, not so much in the author's mind, as in the emotional penumbra of the characters themselves. When it is fused like this, literalness ceases to be literalness — it is merely part of the experience.

If the novel is a form of imaginative art, it cannot be at the same time a vivid and brilliant form of journalism. Out of the teeming, gleaming stream of the present it must select the eternal material of art. There are hopeful signs that some of the younger writers are trying to break away from mere verisimilitude, and, following the development of modern painting, to interpret imaginatively the material and social investiture of their characters; to present their scene by suggestion rather than by enumeration. The higher processes of art are all processes of simplification. The novelist must learn to write, and then he must unlearn it; just as the modern painter learns to draw, and then learns when utterly to disregard his accomplishment, when to subordinate it to a higher and truer effect. In this direction only, it seems to me, can the novel develop into anything more varied and perfect than all the many novels that have gone before.

One of the very earliest American romances might well serve as a suggestion to later writers. In *The Scarlet Letter* how truly in the spirit of art is the mise-en-scène presented. That drudge, the theme-writing high-school student, could scarcely be sent there for information regarding the manners and dress and interiors of Puritan society. The material investiture of the story is presented as if unconsciously; by the reserved, fastidious hand of an artist, not by the gaudy fingers of a showman or the mechanical industry of a department-store window-dresser. As I remember it, in the twilight melancholy of that book, in its consistent mood, one can scarcely see the actual surroundings of the people; one feels them, rather, in the dusk.

Whatever is felt upon the page without being specifically named there — that, one might say, is created. It is the inexplicable presence of the thing not named, of the overtone divined by the ear but not heard by it, the verbal mood, the emotional aura of the fact or the thing or the deed, that gives high quality to the novel or the drama, as well as to poetry itself.

Literalness, when applied to the presenting of mental reactions and of physical sensations, seems to be no more effective than when it is applied to material things. A novel crowded with physical sensations is no less a catalogue than one crowded with furniture. A book like *The Rainbow* by D. H. Lawrence sharply reminds one how vast a distance lies between emotion and mere sensory reactions. Characters can be almost dehumanized by a laboratory study of the behaviour of their bodily organs under sensory stimuli — can be reduced, indeed, to mere animal pulp. Can one imagine anything more terrible than the story of *Romeo and Juliet* rewritten in prose by D. H. Lawrence?

How wonderful it would be if we could throw all the furniture out of the window; and along with it, all the meaningless reiterations concerning physical sensations, all the tiresome old patterns, and leave the room as bare as the stage of a Greek theatre, or as that house into which the glory of Pentecost descended; leave the scene bare for the play of emotions, great and little — for the nursery tale, no less than the tragedy, is killed by tasteless amplitude. The elder Dumas enunciated a great principle when he said that to make a drama, a man needed one passion, and four walls.

Willa Sibert Cather

April 12, 1922

From Not under Forty (*New York: Alfred A. Knopf;* *1936*)

FOUR PREFACES

THE BEST STORIES OF
SARAH ORNE JEWETT

But give to thine own story
Simplicity, with glory.

LOUISE IMOGEN GUINEY

In reading over a package of letters from Sarah
Orne Jewett, I find this observation: "*The thing
that teases the mind over and over for years, and
at last gets itself put down rightly on paper —
whether little or great, it belongs to Literature.*"
Miss Jewett was very conscious of the fact that
when a writer makes anything that belongs to

Four Prefaces

Literature (limiting the term here to imaginative literature, which she of course meant), his material goes through a process very different from that by which he makes merely a good story or a good novel. No one can exactly define this process; but certainly persistence, survival, recurrence in the writer's mind, are highly characteristic of it. The shapes and scenes that have "teased" the mind for years, when they do at last get themselves rightly put down, make a very much higher order of writing, and a much more costly, than the most vivid and vigorous transfer of immediate impressions.

In some of Miss Jewett's earlier books, *Deephaven, Country Byways, Old Friends and New,* one can find first sketches, first impressions, which later crystallized into the almost flawless examples of literary art that make up these two volumes. One can, as it were, watch in process the two kinds of making: the first, which is full of perception and feeling but rather fluid and formless; the second, which is tightly built and significant in design. The design is, indeed, so happy, so right, that it seems inevitable; the design is the story, and the story is the design. The "Pointed Fir" sketches are living things caught in the open, with light and freedom and air-spaces about them. They melt into the land and the life of the land until they are not stories at all, but life itself.

A great many good stories were being written upon New England themes at the same time that Miss Jewett was writing; stories that to many contemporary readers may have seemed more interesting than hers, because they dealt with more startling "situations," were more heavily accented, more elaborately costumed and posed in the studio. But most of them are not very interesting to read and reread today; they have not the one thing that survives all arresting situations, all good writing and clever story-making — inherent, individual beauty; the kind of beauty we feel when a beautiful song is sung by a beautiful voice that is exactly suited to the song.

Pater said that every truly great drama must, in the end, linger in the reader's mind as a sort of ballad. Probably the same thing might be said of every great story. It must leave in the mind of the sensitive reader an intangible residuum of pleasure; a cadence, a quality of voice that is exclusively the writer's own, individual, unique. A quality that one can remember without the volume at hand, can experience over and over again in the mind but can never absolutely define, as one can experience in memory a melody, or the summer perfume of a garden. The magnitude of the subject-matter is not of primary importance, seemingly. An idyll of Theocritus, concerned with sheep and goats and shade and pastures, is today as much alive as the most dramatic passages of the *Iliad* — stirs the reader's feeling quite as much, perhaps, if the reader is a poet.

It is a common fallacy that a writer, if he is talented enough, can achieve this poignant quality by improving upon his subject-matter, using his "imagination" upon it and twisting it to suit his purpose. The truth is that by such a process (which is not imaginative at all!) he can at best produce only a brilliant sham, which, like a badly

The Best Stories of Sarah Orne Jewett

built and pretentious house, looks poor and shabby in a few years. If he achieves anything noble, anything enduring, it must be by giving himself absolutely to his material. And this gift of sympathy is his great gift; it is the fine thing in him that alone can make his work fine. He fades away into the land and people of his heart, he dies of love only to be born again. The artist spends a lifetime in loving the things that haunt him, in having his mind "teased" by them, in trying to get these conceptions down on paper exactly as they are to him and not in conventional poses supposed to reveal their character; trying this method and that, as a painter tries different lightings and different attitudes with his subject to catch the one that presents it more suggestively than any other. And at the end of a lifetime he emerges with much that is more or less happy experimenting, and comparatively little that is the very flower of himself and his genius. I have tried to gather into these two volumes the very best of Miss Jewett's beautiful work: the stories which, read by an eager student fifty years from now, will give him the characteristic flavour, the spirit, the cadence, of an American writer of the first order — and of a New England which will then be a thing of the past.

Even in the stories that fall a little short of being Miss Jewett's finest, there are many delightful characters and there is much beautiful writing. Take, for instance, the first part of "A Second Spring," or the chapter from *Deephaven* called "In Shadow"; or glance at this clear, daybreak passage at the beginning of "By the Morning Boat":

On the coast of Maine, where many green islands and salt inlets fringe the deep-cut shore line; where balsam firs and bayberry bushes send their fragrance far seaward, and song-sparrows sing all day, and the tide runs plashing in and out among the weedy ledges; where cowbells tinkle on the hills, and herons stand in the shady coves — on the lonely coast of Maine stood a small gray house facing the morning light. All the weather-beaten houses of that region face the sea apprehensively, like the women who live in them.

Or consider the closing paragraph of "Marsh Rosemary," which might stand as a tender apology for the art of all new countries, which must grow out of a thin new soil and bear its fate:

Who can laugh at my Marsh Rosemary, or who can cry, for that matter? The gray primness of the plant is made up from a hundred colors if you look close enough to find them. This Marsh Rosemary stands in her own place, and holds her dry leaves and tiny blossoms steadily toward the same sun that the pink lotus blooms for, and the white rose.

The stories chosen for these two volumes vary little in quality, though one may have one's favourites among them. Personally, I like "The Flight of Betsey Lane" better than "The Hiltons' Holiday," though the latter story was especially dear to Miss Jewett herself. I think I know why; that story simply *is the look* — shy, kind, a little wistful — that shines out at one from good country faces on remote farms; it is the look *itself* — and therefore is a little miracle. To have got it down upon the printed page is like bringing the tenderest of early spring flowers from the deep wood into the hot light of summer noon without brusing its petals. The story "William's Wedding" was uncompleted at the time of Miss Jewett's death, and while all the essentials of the picture are there, the writing is in places a little vague, lacks the last co-ordinating touch of the writer's hand.

To note an artist's limitations is but to define his genius. A reporter can write equally well about everything that is presented to his view, but a creative writer can do his best only with what lies within the range and character of his talent. These stories of Miss Jewett's have much to do with fisher-folk and seaside villages; with juniper pastures and lonely farms, neat grey country houses and delightful, well-seasoned old men and women. That, when one thinks of it in a flash, is New England. I remember hearing an English actor say that until he made a motor trip through New England he had supposed that the Americans killed their aged in some merciful fashion, for he saw none in the cities where he played.

There are many kinds of people in the State of Maine, and its neighbouring States, who are not in Miss Jewett's books. There may be Othellos and Iagos and Don Juans, but they are not highly characteristic of the country, they do not come up spontaneously in the juniper pastures as the everlasting does. Miss Jewett wrote of the people who grew out of the soil and the life of the country near her heart, not about exceptional individuals at war with their environment. This was not a creed with her, but an instinctive preference. She once laughingly told me that her head was full of dear old houses and dear old women, and that when an old house and an old woman came together in her brain with a click, she knew that a story was under way.

Born within the scent of the sea, but not within sight of it, in a beautiful old house full of strange and lovely things brought home from all over the globe by seafaring ancestors, she spent much of her girlhood driving about the country with her doctor father on his professional rounds among the farms. She early learned to love her country for what it was. What is quite as important, she saw it as it was. She happened to have the right nature, the right temperament, to see it so — and to understand by intuition the deeper meaning of all she saw.

She had not only the eye, she had the ear. From childhood she must have treasured up those pithy bits of local speech, of native idiom, which enrich and enliven her pages. The language her people speak to each other is a native tongue. No writer can invent it. It is made in the hard school of experience, in communities where language has been undisturbed long enough to take on colour and character from the nature and experiences of the people. The "sayings" of a community, its proverbs, are its characteristic comment upon life; they imply its history, suggest its attitude toward the world, and its way of accepting life. Such an idiom makes the finest language any writer can have; and he can never get it with a notebook. He himself must be able to think and feel in that speech — it is a gift from heart to heart.

Much of Miss Jewett's delightful humour comes from her delicate and tactful handling of this native language of the waterside and country-side, never overdone, never pushed a shade too far; from this, and from her own fine attitude toward her subject-matter. This attitude in itself, though unspoken, is everywhere felt, and constitutes one of the most potent elements of grace and charm in her stories. She had with her own stories and her own characters a very charming relation; spirited, gay, tactful, noble in its essence and a little arch in its expression. In this particular relationship many of our most gifted writers are unfortunate. If a writer's attitude toward his characters and his scene is as vulgar as a showman's, as mercenary as an auctioneer's, vulgar and meretricious will his product for ever remain.

Gilbert Murray has illustrated the two kinds of

beauty in writing by a happy similitude. There is a kind of beauty, he says, which comes from rich ornamentation; like the splendour one might admire on a Chinese junk, gorgeously gilded and painted, hung with rich embroideries and tapestries. Then there is the beauty of a modern yacht, where there is no ornamentation at all; our whole sensation of pleasure in watching a yacht under sail comes from the fact that every line of the craft is designed for one purpose, that everything about it furthers that purpose, so that it has an organic, living simplicity and directness. This, he says, is the beauty for which the Greek writers strove; it is certainly that for which Miss Jewett strove.

If I were asked to name three American books which have the possibility of a long, long life, I would say at once: *The Scarlet Letter, Huckleberry Finn,* and *The Country of the Pointed Firs.* I can think of no others that confront time and change so serenely. The last book seems to me fairly to shine with the reflection of its long, joyous future. It is so tightly yet so lightly built, so little encumbered with heavy materialism that deteriorates and grows old-fashioned. I like to think with what pleasure, with what a sense of rich discovery, the young student of American literature in far distant years to come will take up this book and say: "A masterpiece!" as proudly as if he himself had made it. It will be a message to the future, a message in a universal language, like the tuft of meadow flowers in Robert Frost's fine poem, which the mower abroad in the early morning left standing, just skirted by the scythe, for the mower of the afternoon to gaze upon and wonder at — the one message that even the scythe of Time spares.

February 1925

Written as a preface to the Mayflower Edition of The Best Short Stories of Sarah Orne Jewett (*Boston: Houghton Mifflin; 1925*), which were selected and arranged by Willa Cather.
Incorporated in part in the essay "Miss Jewett" in Not under Forty (*New York: Alfred A. Knopf; 1936*).

GERTRUDE HALL'S

THE WAGNERIAN ROMANCES

I know of only two books in English on the Wagnerian operas that are at all worthy of their subject; Bernard Shaw's *The Perfect Wagnerite* and
The Wagnerian Romances by Gertrude Hall. For
the most part "guides to the opera" are written by
very unintelligent people, who know little about
writing and even less about opera. This book of
Miss Hall's is beautifully written, and the writer
is a discerning critic who has spent her life among
musicians of the first rank. The Wagnerian music-

Gertrude Hall's The Wagnerian Romances

dramas, indeed, have been a part of her life, and she has closely followed the work of the best conductors and interpreters of German opera here and abroad. All these facts might be true of a dull writer, of course. This book is good — so good as to be unique among its kind — because the writer has the rare gift of being able to reproduce the emotional effect of the Wagner operas upon the printed page; to suggest the setting, the scenic environment, the dramatic action, the personality of the characters. Moreover, she is able, in a way all her own, to suggest the character of the music itself.

I first came upon this book when I was staying in a thinly peopled part of the Southwest, far enough from the Metropolitan Opera House. I first read the chapter on *Parsifal*, with increasing delight. I was astonished to find how vividly it recalled to me all the best renderings of that opera I had ever heard. Just the right word was said to start the music going in one's memory, as if one had heard the themes given out on a piano. The essay recalled the scenes, the personages of the drama, and the legendary beauty, the truly religious feeling that haunts it from end to end. I next turned to *The Master-Singers of Nuremberg* and it seemed to me that the rich life of that old German city and the joyous comedy of the piece have seldom stood out on any stage as it did on these pages.

What Miss Hall does, it seems to me, is to reproduce the emotional effect of one art through the medium of another art. This, of course, can scarcely be done in the case of a symphony or a sonata; efforts to do it are usually unsuccessful and often ludicrous. But opera is a hybrid art,—partly literary to begin with. It happens that in the Wagnerian music-drama the literary part of the work is not trivial, as it is so often in operas, but is truly the mate of the music, done by the same hand. The music is throughout concerned with words, and with things that can be presented in language; with human beings and their passions and sorrows, and with places and with periods of time, with particular rivers and particular mountains, even;—with Nuremberg, even.

Gertrude Hall's The Wagnerian Romances

All this feeling for places and the character of landscape and architecture is, in the hands of the right person, readily translatable into words.

I have used the word "translate"; what horrid deeds that word has been made to cover where the Wagnerian operas are concerned! What a frightful jargon Tristan and Isolde speak to each other in the "authorized libretto," what insulting expletives Siegfried and Brünnhilde shout at each other on the rock! Miss Hall, in her introduction, says she respects the libretto-makers for having managed to fit their verse-rendering to the extremely difficult music in any way whatsoever. But in her rendering of the text the right word does not have to come in for the right beat. She is free to make a noble passage of the German into noble English. In the dialogue, when the characters are singing to each other, she translates Wagner's own text most effectively and sympathetically into English prose. Miss Hall is an accomplished linguist, and German is the language in which she is, musically, most at home. All the dialogue in these chapters is Wagner's own, exquisitely done into English, — English that has everywhere the right shading; the right shading for the god, the right shading for the gnome. I know of no other English rendering of Wagner's poems that has anything of the character of the original, — any character at all, for that matter. And the words are here not divorced from the action, but vividly accompanied by the action (in narrative) as Wagner meant them to be. A mere literal translation of the written scene in which Walther for the first time sings before the Master-Singers, for instance, means very little. And the words of Walther's song, literally translated, without the feeling of the accompanying actions, mean almost nothing. Miss Hall's rendering of that scene is a brilliant piece of virtuosity. She builds it up, with its influences and counter-influences, themes and counter-themes, very much as the music itself is built up. If you wish to know how difficult it is to transfer the feeling of an operatic scene upon a page of narrative, try it! I had to attempt it once, in the course of a novel, and I paid Miss Hall the highest compliment one writer can pay another; I stole from her.

I have a great many friends who live in distant parts of the country where operas are not given. I believe that after they have read these chapters on the *Ring of the Nibelungs* they will have got a great deal of the beauty of the cycle. Those who are able to spell out parts of the score on the piano will get just so much more. I am deeply interested in the revival of this book by a publisher who will give it a wide audience, because I know it will give great pleasure to many friends of mine, and to great numbers of people who have the intelligence to appreciate the Wagner operas but not the opportunity to hear them. There are innumerable Women's Clubs, for instance, who take a sort of silent course in music, and conscientiously read the dull books that have been written about operas. When they read this book, they will get, not some foolish facts, but an emotional experience of Wagner's Romances, of those noble, mysterious, significant dramas in roughly made verse. And persons who have heard the operas sung, and beautifully sung, many times, but who are now living in remote places, will find this book potent in reviving their recollections; the scenes will float before them, as they did before me in the blue air of New Mexico when I first made the acquaintance of these delicately suggestive pages.

April 1925

Written as a preface to The Wagnerian Romances *by Gertrude Hall (New York: Alfred A. Knopf; 1925).*

STEPHEN CRANE'S

WOUNDS IN THE RAIN AND
OTHER IMPRESSIONS OF WAR

The sketches in this volume are most of them low-pressure writing, done during, or soon after, Crane's illness in Cuba. He hadn't the vitality to make stories, to pull things together into a sharp design — though "The Price of the Harness" just misses being a fine war story. In one of them the writing is rather commonplace, the sketch "God Rest Ye, Merry Gentlemen" — the only story of Crane's I know which seems distinctly old-fashioned. It is done in an outworn manner that was considered smart in the days when Richard Harding Davis was young, and the war correspondent and his "kit" was a romantic figure. This sketch indulges in a curiously pompous kind of humour which seemed very swagger then:

"He was hideously youthful and innocent and unaware."

"Walkley departed tearlessly for Jamaica, soon after he had bestowed upon his friends much tinned goods and blankets."

"But they departed joyfully before the sun was up and passed into Siboney."

They always departed in that school of writing, they never went anywhere. This chesty manner, doubtless, came in with Kipling. When one re-reads the young Kipling it seems a little absurd, but it still seems to belong. After it became a general affectation, however, it was surely one of the most foolish of literary fashions. But only this one of Crane's war sketches is much tainted by the war-correspondent idiom of the times. In the

Stephen Crane's Wounds in the Rain

others he wrote better than the people of his day, and he wrote like himself. The fact that there is not much design, that these are for the most part collections of impressions which could be arranged as well in one way as another, gives one a chance to examine the sentences, which are part, but only part, of the material out of which stories are made.

When you examine the mere writing in this unorganized material, you see at once that Crane was one of the first post-impressionists; that he began it before the French painters began it, or at least as early as the first of them. He simply knew from the beginning how to handle detail. He estimated it at its true worth — made it serve his purpose and felt no further responsibility about it. I doubt whether he ever spent a laborious half-hour in doing his duty by detail — in enumerating, like an honest, grubby auctioneer. If he saw one thing that engaged him in a room, he mentioned it. If he saw one thing in a landscape that thrilled him, he put it on paper, but he never tried to make a faithful report of everything else within his field of vision, as if he were a conscientious salesman making out his expense-account. ("The red sun was pasted in the sky like a wafer," that careless observation which Mr. Hergesheimer admires so much, isn't exceptional with Crane. He wrote like that when he was writing well.) What about the clouds, and the light on the hills, and the background, and the foreground? Well, Crane left that for his successors to write, and they have been doing it ever since: accounting for everything, as trustees of an estate are supposed to do — thoroughly good business methods applied to art; "doing" landscapes and interiors like house-decorators, putting up the curtains and tacking down the carpets.

Perhaps it was because Stephen Crane had read so little, was so slightly acquainted with the masterpieces of fiction, that he felt no responsibility to be accurate or painstaking in accounting for things and people. He is rather the best of our writers in what is called "description" because he is the least describing. Cuba didn't tempt him to transfer tropical landscapes to paper, any more than New York State had tempted him to do his duty by the countryside.

"The day wore down to the Cuban dusk. . . . The sun threw his last lance through the foliage. The steep mountain-range on the right turned blue and as without detail as a curtain. The tiny ruby of light ahead meant that the ammunition guard were cooking their supper." Enough, certainly. He didn't follow the movement of troops there much more literally than he had in *The Red Badge of Courage*. He knew that the movement of troops was the officers' business, not his. He was in Cuba to write about soldiers and soldiering, and he did; often something like this:

"With his heavy roll of blanket and the half of a shelter tent crossing his right shoulder and under his left arm, each man presented the appearance of being clasped from behind, wrestler-fashion, by a pair of thick white arms.

"There was something distinctive in the way they carried their rifles. There was the grace of the old hunter somewhere in it, the grace of a man whose rifle has become absolutely a part of himself. Furthermore, almost every blue shirt-sleeve was rolled to the elbow, disclosing fore-arms of almost incredible brawn. The rifles seemed light, almost fragile, in the hands that were at the end of those arms, never fat but always rolling with muscles and veins that seemed on the point of bursting."

That is much more to his purpose than what these men were about. That is important, all of it — and that sense of the curious smallness of rifle-butts in the hands of regulars is most important of all.

The most interesting things in the bundle of impressions called "War Memories" are the death of Surgeon Gibbs, Crane's observations about the regulars, "the men," and his admiration for Admiral Sampson. Sometimes when a man is writing carelessly, without the restraint he puts upon himself when he is in good form, one can surprise some of his secrets and read rather more than he perhaps intended. He admired Sampson because he wasn't like the time-honoured conception of a bluff seaman. "It is his distinction not to resemble the preconceived type of his standing. When I first met him he seemed immensely bored by the war and with the command of the North Atlantic Squadron. I perceived a manner, where I thought I perceived a mood, a point of view."

He admired the Admiral because he wasn't theatrical, detested noise and show.

"No bunting, no arches, no fireworks; nothing but the perfect management of a big fleet. That is a record for you. No trumpets, no cheers of the populace. Just plain, pure, unsauced accomplishment. But ultimately he will reap his reward in — in what? In text-books on sea campaigns. No more. The people choose their own, and they choose the kind they like. Who has a better right? Anyhow, he is a great man. And when you are once started you can continue to be a great man without the help of bouquets and banquets."

And that point of view caused Mr. Crane's biographer no little trouble. He himself managed so conspicuously to elude the banquets and bouquets of his own calling that he left a very meagre tradition among "literary people." Had he been more expansive at coffee-houses and luncheon clubs where his art was intelligently discussed, had he even talked about his own tales among a few friends, or written a few papers about his works for reviews, what a convenience for Thomas Beer! But there is every evidence that he was a reticent and unhelpful man, with no warmhearted love of giving out opinions. His ideal, apparently, was "just plain, pure, unsauced accomplishment."

January 1926

From The Work of Stephen Crane, *Volume IX* (*New York: Alfred A. Knopf; 1926*).

DEFOE'S

THE FORTUNATE MISTRESS

Defoe was writing *Roxanna, or, The Fortunate Mistress* in 1720, twenty years before Richardson produced *Pamela*. He was a writer in much the same sense that he was a hosier, and drove both trades as well as he could. A practical journalist, he wrote on politics, commerce, religion, publishing in pamphlets because there was no periodic press. When he was past fifty, and had been writing all his life, he discovered that there was a much larger public for narratives than for political articles. The success of *Robinson Crusoe* astonished him, and he decided to follow a winning lead. His family expenses were heavy, he was burdened with marriageable daughters, and his hosiery business in London was not flourishing enough to provide portions for them. Stories, he saw, could be made to pay better than either hose or instructive pamphlets.

The material for *Robinson Crusoe* Defoe came upon by chance — by one of those chances which are always happening to the born journalist. He met Alexander Selkirk at the house of a friend in Bristol, and got the story of the shipwrecked man's adventures from his own lips. Selkirk afterward declared that he had handed over his papers to this sympathetic listener. Defoe's literal method never worked out so well again as in *Robinson Crusoe* — at least, not for readers of our time. Robinson, like all his other heroes, lived by his wits, but since he practised his ingenuity upon a desert island and the untamed forces of nature, the details are not so revolting as in the narratives in which the hero uses his wits upon the persons and pocketbooks of his fellow mortals. Moreover, since Robinson has the scene to himself, the modern reader does not miss so much the thousand flowers of courtesy and sympathy and fine feeling he has come to expect in the narrative that deals with human intercourse.

Defoe was upwards of sixty when he began *The Fortunate Mistress:* the story of a daughter of French Protestant parents who fled to England in 1683, married at fifteen to a London brewer, with whom she lives for more than eight years and by whom she has five children. The husband dissipates his own fortune and hers in drinking and hunting, finally deserts her, and goes abroad to enlist in foreign military service. Young and handsome, with five children, no money, and many debts, Roxanna is left to shift for herself — and she demonstrates that she is mightily competent to do so. She embarks almost at once upon a career which it would be absurdly euphuistic to call a career of amatory adventure. A life of adventure it certainly is, though the adventure is always the same. The monetary gains vary somewhat in her various engagements, but they are always large. Defoe undertook to tell the story of a fortunate mistress, one who concerned herself only with men of quality, wealth, and boundless good nature; one who managed her affairs successfully and practised her profession with good sense, shrewdness, and economy until she was well past fifty.

Roxanna's story is told by herself; the entire novel is written in the first person, the fortunate mistress being the narrator. She leaves nothing untold, and there is much to relate. Her story ought to be absorbingly interesting, but it is only inversely so. The most interesting thing about it is that, with such a warehouse of inflammatory material to draw from, it remains so dull.

Here we have the novel (or we may be academic and call it the "romance"), stripped to its bare bones; and what have we? It happens to be much easier to say what we have not. Defoe is a writer of ready invention but no imagination — with none of the personal attributes which, fused together somehow, make imagination. His narrative runs smoothly, evenly, convincingly; the best thing about it is his vigorous, unornamented English. There is a strong weave in the sentences as they follow each other that gives pleasure to the eye, as the feel of good hand-woven linen does to the fingertips. But after a while one demands something more. There is never a change of tempo, never a modulation of voice, or a quickening of sympathy. The episodes of Roxanna's narrative never emerge from the level text and become "scenes." Fifty years before Defoe, Bunyan had written much of *The Pilgrim's Progress* in scenes of the most satisfying kind; where little is said but much is felt and communicated: one has only to recall the delightful episodes of Christiana's sojourn at the House Beautiful, or Mercy's descent into the Valley of Humiliation. The "scene" in fiction is not a mere matter of construction, any more than it is in life. When we have a vivid experience in social intercourse, pleasant or unpleasant, it records itself in our memory in the form of a scene; and when it flashes back to us, all sorts of apparently unim-

Four Prefaces

portant details are flashed back with it. When a writer has a strong or revelatory experience with his characters, he unconsciously creates a scene; gets a depth of picture, and writes, as it were, in three dimensions instead of two. The absence of these warm and satisfying moments in any work of fiction is final proof of the author's poverty of emotion and lack of imagination.

There are no scenes in Roxanna's narrative, and there is no atmosphere. Her adventures in France are exactly like those in England; one is not conscious of the slightest change in her surroundings or way of living. Defoe had travelled, and so does his heroine. But all countries and all cities are alike to Roxanna, just as all well-to-do men are alike to her. When she is touring with her French Prince, she goes to Venice for her "lying-in" — but it is all one with Spitalfields. The child died after two months, and she says that she was on the whole not sorry, considering the inconvenience of travelling with an infant. About the city itself, or her way of living there, she does not drop a remark. While one may much prefer this reticence to the travelogue school of fiction, it certainly adds to the evidence of a curious insensibility in Roxanna and her author. The whole book, indeed, is a mass of evidence upon that point, and that is its chief interest. The reader gets no impression of Roxanna's physical surroundings at any time; her houses and retinues in England, France, and Holland are mere names. The only things in her material investiture which interest either her or her creator are her clothes. She does enumerate at some length the gowns and jewels the Prince bought for her — enumerates them more like a merchant taking stock than like a pretty woman describing her costumes. We are never told anything so foolish as that the Prince liked her in this or that. One can say this for Roxanna: she is never sentimental.

There are no scenes in this novel, there is no atmosphere, no picturing of rooms or gardens or household gear which for one reason or another were dear to the narrator — as a particular cushion is dear to a cat, or a corner by the fire to a dog. There is no conversation, or almost none.

Four Prefaces

Talk is used chiefly to present arguments. While conversation was slow to develop in the English novel, there is living human intercourse through conversation in *The Pilgrim's Progress*, and many of the theological discussions between Christian and Faithful are more lively and full of feeling than any of Roxanna's dialogues with her lovers.

Roxanna had enough sense of character for her purpose. Of her hard-riding, hard-drinking first husband she paints a good picture; one gets a sense of the man's personality. Her maid, the sprightly and resourceful Amy, the companion and sharer of her adventures, is, after Roxanna herself, the most living person in the book. In discussing her lovers, our heroine is concerned with only one quality, their generosity. When she deigns to be personal, her strokes tell, and one does manage to find out something about these men beyond the ample provision they made for Roxanna. If she and her author had not been so blind to everything but francs and pounds, they might have passed on a good deal to us.

As against so many things that are absent from

Defoe's The Fortunate Mistress

Defoe's story, one thing is amazingly, powerfully, unflaggingly present: verisimilitude. From the first paragraph one never doubts that this is a woman's actual story, told by a woman. The author never gets outside his character, never insinuates anything through her, has no feelings about her beyond those she has about herself. The reader forgets Daniel Defoe altogether; he is reading a woman's autobiography. And what a woman! One cannot imagine the most starved little girl drudge, in the cruelest age of domestic service, if this book had fallen into her hands, lingering wistfully over its pages and coveting Roxanna's Prince or her diamonds. One cannot believe that the most mush-headed boy would long to take her over from the Prince. The starved and the mush-headed are romantic; they want what goes with the Prince and the diamonds, they believe in their own capacity for pleasure. But Defoe and Roxanna knew well enough that they had none, and no more unromantic pair ever got themselves into print. Their great, their saving quality is that they do not try to be what they are not, and never for a moment pretend to any of the fine feelings they do not possess. This mental integrity makes the narrative, as a piece of writing, almost flawless; as self-sufficient as a column of figures correctly added. Lewd situations are dispatched without lewdness. The book is as safe as sterilized gauze. One is bumped up smartly against the truth, old enough but always new, that in novels, as in poetry, the facts are nothing, the feeling is everything.

Open any volume of M. Fabre's studies of insect life, and one can find passages about the life-struggle of beetles, the love-makings and domestic cares of ants or grasshoppers, passages that are so warm and rich and full of colour, so full of wisdom and humour and the sense of tragedy and beauty, that they make poor Roxanna, with her thirty years of profitable engagements, seem not animal, but mineral. With Fabre, the poetic Provençal was always getting the better of the scientist. When the lights are put out, and the moths he has vainly enticed for weeks at last come flying through the summer night to court the lady under a gauze tent on his study table, it is Fabre, and his breathless children, hidden in the dark, who have the romance and the adventure, not the moths. And they have more in their silent half-hour than Defoe is able to beat up for Roxanna and her dozen lovers in five hundred pages. M. Fabre is much more wonderful than his insects; but Defoe is not at all more remarkable than Roxanna. They are both most remarkable in that, lacking all the most valuable gifts a writer can have except one, they made themselves an immortal place in English, in European, literature.

Defoe seems to have had only one deep interest, and that was in making a living. Read *The Complete British Tradesman* and marvel at how intensely, how acutely, every mean device and petty economy appealed to him; how every stingy trim, every possible twist and sharp practice in shopkeeping and servant-grinding, stirred him and gratified him. All the misers in fiction are sentimental, inexpert, and unresourceful, judged by the standards advocated in this work written for the guidance of Defoe's fellow tradesmen. It is one of the meanest and most sordid books ever written. It makes one ashamed of being human.

Defoe was concerned not only about the matter of making his own living, he was intensely interested in the way other people made theirs; in all the shifts by which we feed and clothe ourselves, and buy a business and get together a property. It must have been much harder to wring a livelihood from a stony world then than it is now: in the profound concern of this small, mean, vigorous spirit, we get some aching sense of the cruel pressure of the times.

In one book Defoe's single theme was quite enough. It happened that the way in which Robinson Crusoe made a living was extremely interesting: nearly everyone would like to try it for a month or two. Except for the moralizing, which few of us read, Defoe's immortal work is an account of how Robinson maintained himself and acquired property on a desert island.

The Fortunate Mistress is an account of how a woman maintained herself and acquired property

— and her way of doing it is not interesting. Her profession, of course, is an old theme in art; and of the queens of that profession great artists have left portraits of enduring beauty in sculpture and painting and literature. But such a theme, in the hands of Roxanna and that thrifty hosier, Daniel Defoe — ! Shakespeare himself could never have created two such characters; he wouldn't have had the patience. They remind us of what Heine said, that no irony can compete with God's irony.

Some sentimental critics, of the kind that Defoe himself called "high-flying," have tried to make out a case for *The British Tradesman* as a masterpiece of irony. Its author would have said that you might as well call the multiplication table irony. Defoe attempted ironical treatment more than once, in imitation of Swift, but he could never sustain that mood for long. He was as devoid of humour as he was of idealism, of romance, and of geniality. *Robinson Crusoe* and *The Fortunate Mistress* splendidly illustrate to what different ends a writer can put the same

Four Prefaces

talent. The one book has what Stevenson called charm of circumstance, the other emphatically has not; but in both the same nature is effectively asserting itself; mean enough and vital enough — invulnerable because it never affects qualities which it neither comprehends nor admires.

Written as an introduction to the Borzoi Classics edition of this book (New York: Alfred A. Knopf; 1924).

MY FIRST NOVELS

[*There Were Two*]

MY FIRST NOVELS

[*There Were Two*]

My first novel, *Alexander's Bridge*, was very like what painters call a studio picture. It was the result of meeting some interesting people in London. Like most young writers, I thought a book should be made out of "interesting material," and at that time I found the new more exciting than the familiar. The impressions I tried to communicate on paper were genuine, but they were very shallow. I still find people who like that book because it follows the most conventional pattern,

My First Novels

and because it is more or less laid in London. London is supposed to be more engaging than, let us say, Gopher Prairie; even if the writer knows Gopher Prairie very well and London very casually. Soon after the book was published I went for six months to Arizona and New Mexico. The longer I stayed in a country I really did care about, and among people who were a part of the country, the more unnecessary and superficial a book like *Alexander's Bridge* seemed to me. I did no writing down there, but I recovered from the conventional editorial point of view.

When I got back to Pittsburgh I began to write a book entirely for myself; a story about some Scandinavians and Bohemians who had been neighbours of ours when I lived on a ranch in Nebraska, when I was eight or nine years old. I found it a much more absorbing occupation than writing *Alexander's Bridge*; a different process altogether. Here there was no arranging or "inventing"; everything was spontaneous and took its own place, right or wrong. This was like taking a ride through a familiar country on a horse that knew the way, on a fine morning when you felt like riding. The other was like riding in a park, with someone not altogether congenial, to whom you had to be talking all the time. Since I wrote this book for myself, I ignored all the situations and accents that were then generally thought to be necessary. The "novel of the soil" had not then come into fashion in this country. The drawing-room was considered the proper setting for a novel, and the only characters worth reading about were smart people or clever people. "O. Henry" had made the short story go into the world of the cheap boarding-house and the shop-girl and the truck-driver. But Henry James and Mrs. Wharton were our most interesting novelists, and most of the younger writers followed their manner, without having their qualifications.

O Pioneers! interested me tremendously, because it had to do with a kind of country I loved, because it was about old neighbours, once very dear, whom I had almost forgotten in the hurry and excitement of growing up and finding out what the world was like and trying to get on in it. But I did not in the least expect that other people would see anything in a slow-moving story, without "action," without "humour," without a "hero"; a story concerned entirely with heavy farming people, with cornfields and pasture lands and pig yards, — set in Nebraska, of all places! As everyone knows, Nebraska is distinctly déclassé as a literary background; its very name throws the delicately atuned critic into a clammy shiver of embarrassment. Kansas is almost as unpromising. Colorado, on the contrary, is considered quite possible. Wyoming really has some class, of its own kind, like well-cut riding breeches. But a New York critic voiced a very general opinion when he said: "I simply don't care a damn what happens in Nebraska, no matter who writes about it."

O Pioneers! was not only about Nebraska farmers; the farmers were Swedes! At that time, 1912, the Swede had never appeared on the printed page in this country except in broadly

My First Novels

humorous sketches; and the humour was based on two peculiarities: his physical strength, and his inability to pronounce the letter "j." I had certainly good reasons for supposing that the book I had written for myself would remain faithfully with me, and continue to be exclusively my property. I sent it to Mr. Ferris Greenslet, of Houghton Mifflin, who had published *Alexander's Bridge*, and was truly astonished when he wrote me they would publish it.

I was very much pleased when William Heinemann decided to publish it in England. I had met Mr. Heinemann in London several times, when I was on the editorial staff of *McClure's Magazine*, and I had the highest opinion of his taste and judgment. His personal taste was a thing quite apart from his business, and it was uncompromising. The fact that a second-rate book sold tremendously never made him hedge and insist that there must be something pretty good in it after all. Most publishers, like most writers, are ruined by their successes.

My First Novels

When my third book, *The Song of the Lark*, came along, Heinemann turned it down. I had never heard from him directly that he liked *O Pioneers!* but now I had a short hand-written letter from him, telling me that he admired it very much; that he was declining *The Song of the Lark* because he thought in that book I had taken the wrong road, and that the full-blooded method, which told everything about everybody, was not natural to me and was not the one in which I would ever take satisfaction. "As for myself," he wrote, "I always find the friendly, confidential tone of writing of this sort distressingly familiar, even when the subject matter is very fine."

At that time I did not altogether agree with Mr. Heinemann, nor with Randolph Bourne, in this country, who said in his review almost the same thing. One is always a little on the defensive about one's last book. But when the next book, *My Ántonia*, came along, quite of itself and with no direction from me, it took the road of *O Pioneers!* — not the road of *The Song of the Lark*.

My First Novels

Too much detail is apt, like any other form of extravagance, to become slightly vulgar; and it quite destroys in a book a very satisfying element analogous to what painters call "composition."

Written for Part Six of The Colophon, 1931

ON

THE ART OF FICTION

ON

THE ART OF FICTION

One is sometimes asked about the "obstacles" that confront young writers who are trying to do good work. I should say the greatest obstacles that writers today have to get over are the dazzling journalistic successes of twenty years ago, stories that surprised and delighted by their sharp photographic detail and that were really nothing more than lively pieces of reporting. The whole aim of that school of writing was novelty — never a very important thing in art. They gave us, altogether, poor standards — taught us to multiply our ideas instead of to condense them. They tried to make a story out of every theme that occurred to them and to get returns on every situation that suggested itself. They got returns, of a kind. But their work, when one looks back on it, now that the novelty upon which they counted so much is gone, is journalistic and thin. The especial merit of a good reportorial story is that it shall be intensely interesting and pertinent today and shall have lost its point by tomorrow.

Art, it seems to me, should simplify. That, indeed, is very nearly the whole of the higher artistic process; finding what conventions of form and what detail one can do without and yet preserve the spirit of the whole — so that all that one has suppressed and cut away is there to the reader's consciousness as much as if it were in type on the page. Millet had done hundreds of sketches of peasants sowing grain, some of them very complicated and interesting, but when he came to paint the spirit of them all into one picture, "The Sower," the composition is so simple that it

On the Art of Fiction

seems inevitable. All the discarded sketches that went before made the picture what it finally became, and the process was all the time one of simplifying, of sacrificing many conceptions good in themselves for one that was better and more universal.

Any first-rate novel or story must have in it the strength of a dozen fairly good stories that have been sacrificed to it. A good workman can't be a cheap workman; he can't be stingy about wasting material, and he cannot compromise. Writing ought either to be the manufacture of stories for which there is a market demand — a business as safe and commendable as making soap or breakfast foods — or it should be an art, which is always a search for something for which there is no market demand, something new and untried, where the values are intrinsic and have nothing to do with standardized values. The courage to go on without compromise does not come to a writer all at once — nor, for that matter, does the ability. Both are phases of natural development. In the beginning, the artist, like his public, is wedded to old forms, old ideals, and his vision is blurred by the memory of old delights he would like to re-capture.

From The Borzoi 1920 (*New York: Alfred A. Knopf; 1920*).

KATHERINE MANSFIELD

KATHERINE MANSFIELD

Every writer and critic of discernment who looked into Katherine Mansfield's first volume of short stories must have felt that here was a very individual talent. At this particular time few writers care much about their medium except as a means for expressing ideas. But in Katherine Mansfield one recognized virtuosity, a love for the medium she had chosen.

The qualities of a second-rate writer can easily be defined, but a first-rate writer can only be experienced. It is just the thing in him which escapes analysis that makes him first-rate. One can catalogue all the qualities that he shares with other writers, but the thing that is his very own, his timbre, this cannot be defined or explained any more than the quality of a beautiful speaking voice can be.

It was usually Miss Mansfield's way to approach the major forces of life through comparatively trivial incidents. She chose a small reflector to throw a luminous streak out into the shadowy realm of personal relationships. I feel that personal relationships, especially the uncatalogued ones, the seemingly unimportant ones, interested her most. To my thinking, she never measured herself up so fully as in the two remarkable stories about an English family in New Zealand, "Prelude" and "At the Bay."

I doubt whether any contemporary writer has made one feel more keenly the many kinds of personal relations which exist in an everyday "happy family" who are merely going on living their daily lives, with no crises or shocks or bewildering complications to try them. Yet every individual in that household (even the children) is clinging passionately to his individual soul, is in terror of losing it in the general family flavour. As in most families, the mere struggle to have anything of one's own, to be one's self at all, creates an element of strain which keeps everybody almost at the breaking-point.

One realizes that even in harmonious families there is this double life: the group life, which is the one we can observe in our neighbour's household, and, underneath, another — secret and passionate and intense — which is the real life that stamps the faces and gives character to the voices of our friends. Always in his mind each member of these social units is escaping, running away, trying to break the net which circumstances and his own affections have woven about him. One realizes that human relationships are the tragic necessity of human life; that they can never be wholly satisfactory, that every ego is half the time greedily seeking them, and half the time pulling away from them. In those simple relationships of loving husband and wife, affectionate sisters, children and grandmother, there are innumerable shades of sweetness and anguish which make up the pattern of our lives day by day, though they are not down in the list of subjects from which the conventional novelist works.

Katherine Mansfield's peculiar gift lay in her interpretation of these secret accords and antipathies which lie hidden under our everyday behaviour, and which more than any outward events make our lives happy or unhappy. Had she lived, her development would have gone on in this direction more than in any other. When she touches this New Zealand family and those far-away memories ever so lightly, as in "The Doll's House," there is a magic one does not find in the other stories, fine as some of them are. With this theme the very letters on the page become alive. She communicates vastly more than she actually writes. One goes back and runs through the pages to find the text which made one know certain things about Linda or Burnell or Beryl, and the text is not there — but something was there, all the same — is there, though no typesetter will ever set it. It is this overtone. which is too fine for the printing press and comes through without it, that makes one know that this writer had something of the gift which is one of the rarest things in writing, and quite the most precious. That she had not the happiness of developing her powers to the full is sad enough. She wrote the truth from Fontainebleau a few weeks before she died: *"The old mechanism isn't mine any longer, and I can't control the new."* She had lived through the first stage, had outgrown her young art, so that it seemed false to her in comparison with the new light that was breaking within. The "new mechanism," big enough to convey the new knowledge, she had not the bodily strength to set in motion.

Katherine Mansfield's published *Journal* begins in 1914 and ends in 1922, some months before her death. It is the record of a long struggle with illness, made more cruel by lack of money and by the physical hardships that war conditions brought about in England and France. At the age of twenty-two (when most young people have a secret conviction that they are immortal), she was already ill in a Bavarian *pension*. From the time when she left New Zealand and came back to England to make her own way, there was never an interval in which she did not have to drive herself beyond her strength. She never reached the stage when she could work with a relaxed elbow. In her story "Prelude," when the family are moving, and the storeman lifts the little girl into the dray and tucks her up, he says: "Easy does it." She knew this, long afterward, but she never had a chance to put that method into practice. In all her earlier stories there is something fierce about her attack, as if she took up a new tale in the spirit of overcoming it. "Do or die" is the mood, — indeed, she must have faced that alternative more than once: a girl come back to make her living in London, without health or money or influential friends, — with no assets but talent and pride.

In her volume of stories entitled *Bliss*, published in 1920 (most of them had been written some years before and had appeared in periodicals), she throws down her glove, utters her little challenge in the high language which she knew better than did most of her readers:

> *But I tell you, my lord fool, out of this nettle, danger, we pluck this flower, safety.*

A fine attitude, youthful and fiery: out of all the difficulties of life and art we will snatch *something.* No one was ever less afraid of the nettle; she was defrauded unfairly of the physical vigour which seems the natural accompaniment of a high and daring spirit.

At thirteen Katherine Mansfield made the long voyage to England with her grandmother, to go to school in London. At eighteen she returned to her own family in Wellington, New Zealand. It was then the struggle against circumstances began. She afterward burned all her early diaries, but it is those I should have liked to read. Exile may be easy to bear for those who have lived their lives. But at eighteen, after four years of London, to be thrown back into a prosperous commercial colony at the end of the world was starvation.

There is no homesickness and no hunger so unbearable. Many a young artist would sell his future, all his chances, simply to get back to the world where other people are doing the only things that, to his inexperience, seem worth doing at all.

Years afterward, when Katherine Mansfield had begun to do her best work but was rapidly sinking in vitality, her homesickness stretched all the other way — backwards, for New Zealand and that same crude Wellington. Unpromising as it was for her purpose, she felt that it was the only territory she could claim, in the deepest sense, as her own. The *Journal* tells us how often she went back to it in her sleep. She recounts these dreams at some length: but the entry which makes one realize that homesickness most keenly is a short one, made in Cornwall in 1918:

> "*June 20th.* The twentieth of June 1918.
> C'est de la misère.
> Non, pas ça exactement. Il y a quelque chose — une profonde malaise me suive comme un ombre.

Katherine Mansfield

Oh, why write bad French? Why write at all?
11,500 miles are so many — too many by 11,499¾
for me."

Eleven thousand five hundred miles is the distance from England to New Zealand.

By this, 1918, she had served her apprentice-
ship. She had gone through a succession of en-
thusiasms for this master and that, formed friend-
ships with some of the young writers of her own
time. But the person who had freed her from the
self-consciousness and affectations of the experimenting young writer, and had brought her to her
realest self, was not one of her literary friends but,
quite simply, her own brother.

He came over in 1915 to serve as an officer. He
was younger than she, and she had not seen him
for six years. After a short visit with her in London he went to the front, and a few weeks later
was killed in action. But he had brought to his
sister the New Zealand of their childhood, and
out of those memories her best stories were to
grow. For the remaining seven years of her life
(she died just under thirty-five) her brother

seems to have been almost constantly in her mind. A great change comes over her feelings about art; what it is, and why it is. When she prays to become "humble," it is probably the slightly showy quality in the early stories that she begs to be delivered from — and forgiven for. The *Journal* from 1918 on is a record of a readjustment to life, a changing sense of its deepest realities. One of the entries in 1919 recounts a dream in which her brother, "Chummie," came back to her:

> "I hear his hat and stick thrown on to the hall-table. He runs up the stairs, three at a time. 'Hullo, darling!' But I can't move — I can't move. He puts his arm round me, holding me tightly, and we kiss — a long, firm, family kiss. And the kiss means: We are of the same blood; we have absolute confidence in each other; we love; all is well; nothing can ever come between us."

In the same year she writes:

> "Now it is May 1919. Six o'clock. I am sitting in my own room thinking of Mother: I want to cry.

But my thoughts are beautiful and full of gaiety. I think of *our* house, *our* garden, *us* children — the lawn, the gate and Mother coming in. 'Children! Children!' I really only ask for time to write it all."

But she did not find too late the things she cared for most. She could not have written that group of New Zealand stories when she first came to London. There had to be a long period of writing for writing's sake. The spontaneous untutored outpouring of personal feeling does not go very far in art. It is only the practised hand that can make the natural gesture, — and the practised hand has often to grope its way. She tells us that she made four false starts on "At the Bay," and when she finished the story it took her nearly a month to recover.

The *Journal,* painful though it is to read, is not the story of utter defeat. She had not, as she said, the physical strength to write what she now knew were, to her, the most important things in life. But she had found them, she possessed them, her mind fed on them. On them, and on the language

Katherine Mansfield

of her greatest poet. (She read Shakespeare continually, when she was too ill to leave her bed.) The inexhaustible richness of that language seems to have been like a powerful cordial, warmed her when bodily nourishment failed her.

Among the stories she left unfinished there is one of singular beauty, written in the autumn of 1922, a few months before her death, the last piece of work she did. She called it "Six Years After": Linda and Burnell grown old, and the boy six years dead. It has the same powerful slightness which distinguishes the other New Zealand stories, and an even deeper tenderness.

Of the first of the New Zealand stories, "Prelude," Miss Mansfield wrote an answer to the inquiries of an intimate friend:

"This is about as much as I can say about it. You know, if the truth were known, I have a perfect passion for the island where I was born. Well, in the early morning there I always remember feeling that this little island has dipped back into the dark blue sea during the night only to rise again at gleam of day, all hung with bright spangles and glittering drops. (When you ran over the dewy grass you positively felt that your feet tasted salt.) I tried to catch that moment — with something of its sparkle and its flavour. And just as on those mornings white milky mists rise and uncover some beauty, then smother it again and then again disclose it, I tried to lift that mist from my people and let them be seen and then to hide them again. . . . It's so difficult to describe all this and it sounds perhaps over-ambitious and vain."

An unpretentious but very suggestive statement of how an artist sets to work, and of the hazy sort of thing that almost surely lies behind and directs interesting or beautiful design. And not with the slighter talents only. Tolstoi himself, one knows from the different Lives and letters, went to work in very much the same way. The long novels, as well as the short tales, grew out of little family dramas, personal intolerances and predilections, — promptings not apparent to the casual reader and incomprehensible to the commercial novel-maker.

From the essay "Katherine Mansfield," in Not under Forty (*New York: Alfred A. Knopf;* 1936).

LIGHT ON ADOBE WALLS

LIGHT ON ADOBE WALLS

[An unpublished fragment]

Every artist knows that there is no such thing as "freedom" in art. The first thing an artist does when he begins a new work is to lay down the barriers and limitations; he decides upon a certain composition, a certain key, a certain relation of creatures or objects to each other. He is never free, and the more splendid his imagination, the more intense his feeling, the farther he goes from general truth and general emotion. Nobody can paint the sun, or sunlight. He can only paint the tricks that shadows play with it, or what it does to forms. He cannot even paint those relations of light and shade — he can only paint some emotion they give him, some man-made arrangement of them that happens to give him personal delight — a conception of clouds over distant mesas (or over the towers of St. Sulpice) that makes one nerve in him thrill and tremble. At bottom all he can give you is the thrill of his own poor little nerve — the projection in paint of a fleeting pleasure in a certain combination of form and colour, as temporary and almost as physical as a taste on the tongue. This oft-repeated pleasure in a painter becomes of course a "style," a way of seeing and feeling things, a favourite mood. What could be more different than Leonardo's treatment of daylight, and Velasquez'? Light is pretty much the same in Italy and Spain — southern light. Each man painted what he got out of light — what it did to him.

No art can do anything at all with great natural forces or great elemental emotions. No poet can write of love, hate, jealousy. He can only touch these things as they affect the people in his drama and his story, and unless he is more interested in his own little story and his foolish little people than in the Preservation of the Indian or Sex or Tuberculosis, then he ought to be working in a laboratory or a bureau.

Art is a concrete and personal and rather childish thing after all — no matter what people do to graft it into science and make it sociological and psychological; it is no good at all unless it is let alone to be itself — a game of make-believe, of re-production, very exciting and delightful to people who have an ear for it or an eye for it. Art is too terribly human to be very "great," perhaps. Some very great artists have outgrown art, the men were bigger than the game. Tolstoi did, and Leonardo did. When I hear the last opuses, I think Beethoven did. Shakespeare died at fifty-three, but there is an awful veiled threat in *The Tempest* that he too felt he had outgrown his toys, was about to put them away and free that spirit of Comedy and Lyrical Poetry and all the rest he held captive — quit play-making and verse-making for ever and turn his attention — to what, he did not hint, but it was probably merely to enjoy with all his senses that Warwickshire country which he loved to weakness — with a warm physical appetite. But he died before he had tried to grow old, never became a bitter old man wrangling with abstractions or creeds. . . .